"LADIES: HERE'S WHY YOU KEEP CHOOSING THE WRONG GUY"

GOD Bless!

Paul Bryant

Copyright © 2016 Paul Bryant

All rights reserved.

ISBN: 153056929X
ISBN-13: 978-1530569298

DEDICATION

This book is dedicated to women everywhere.

CONTENTS

	Introduction	vi
1	Men are Fishers	1
2	Sights Set	9
3	The Wounded Animal	16
4	Power Struggle	22
5	The Aggressive Woman	26
6	Men vs. Women	31
7	Courting not Dating	34
8	Long way to a Designed Destination	41
9	Real Men	44
10	7 Quick Tips	48

INTRODUCTION

As a boy growing up in a house with three women helped me understand both sides of the coin. I understand what women want from men and what men need from women. It's funny that today the roles in relationships have changed drastically from what I remember as a kid. It was almost an unwritten rule that men were to be leaders, to provide and to protect. The family and women were to be more of the helpmeet and support for the man.

However, today it seems that men have become more of the helpmeet and women are the ones that lead, provide and protect. I understand that change is forever and nothing stays the same but I also believe there are some principles that should forever be constant undisturbed systems that follow us into eternity. In other words I feel that relationships should still function like they did when I was growing up, and that's the man leading, providing and protecting the family. I meet women all the time who say "A good man is nowhere to be found." Many say

"Where are all the good men?" I really believe that there are a lot of good men that still exist. They are looking for the right woman. I think that the problem is more of a major lowering of standards that has pushed men into an unknown territory of receiving all of the benefits of a relationship without having to put in any real work. Men once knew that in order to receive certain benefits from a woman it was going to take time, a lot of effort and some chasing. This was understood among men so they were prepared to put in the work. But over the years the standards that women once had have been reduced and the work that men use to have to put in has turned into a simple dinner and a movie. Just like that it's over, a few butterflies in the stomach and the benefits that used to come over time now happen in one night.

When the standards were lowered I believe a lot of good men were caught up in the new rule of dating and relationships. So as the standard has been lowered by a lot of women the expectation of a chase and work has also been lowered for men. Men have now become accustomed to putting in halfhearted efforts with one or maybe even two women at a time with the goal of sex before any kind of intimacy let alone marriage. I understand that this lowering of standards is not the case for every woman. Fortunately there are still a lot of women that stand by the old school values of courting and marriage.

There is a problem however, when there are so many women who don't hold those same values it draws a lot of men away from the good women, who still believe in being pursued. The good women lose out because the women with lower standards are willing to give everything away at "hello." I do believe there is still hope for you women who believe in the old-fashioned way of doing things.

One thing about society is that it continues to lower its morals.

As things begin to get more acceptable, it becomes easier for the man. This new hassle free way of dating eventually becomes old from all the one night, two night and one week stands. Men eventually begin to miss the chase, work and the reward of conquering women. In this book I want to help women understand the mindset of a good man as well as determine if a man is fishing for fun, food or for the sport. All men are fishers but it's the job of you the woman to detect which type of fisher comes into your life. I will have a chapter dedicated to this topic. I also want to help women by providing some important do's and dont's when pursuing a relationship that will help you avoid a lot of traps set by the wrong man. These tips will also help you become more successful in identifying the man that has been set aside especially for you. There is a good man out there for you. My hope is that this book is a tool to help you identify this man when he comes into your life. I believe it will also help you to avoid a lot of wasted time and frustration that occurs from putting in unnecessary effort with the wrong man.

Let's go!

CHAPTER 1
MEN ARE FISHERS

Men are like hunters, we love the thrill of the chase and capture. Hunting is actually a part of our nature. I like to put men in the category of fishermen. All men fish, we either are fishing for fun, food or sport. Most men who fish already have an idea of what type of fish they are going after that day before they even leave their house. Most of the time they have already chosen the specific bait they want to use. The right equipment, the best fishing spot and whether or not the fish they want are biting at that particular location. As I mentioned earlier there are three types of fishermen.

The first type I want to talk about is the guy who fishes for fun. This guy goes after women with no intention whatsoever of having any type of committed relationship. He's just out for the thrill of the moment, the one night stand. This type of fisher is usually the one who catches the fish and brings it to the rest of his friends on the boat to brag about his catch. How big her bottom may be, how hard it was for him to catch her, the type of bait he used to capture the fish and the good time he had in the process. Then he takes a picture with the fish (for social media) and throws her back into the water because after all he's fishing for fun. He never had any intention of keeping the fish at all. How do you as a woman detect if the man that has just approached you is just fishing for fun?

Most of the time these guys don't want any real conversation. They usually try to keep the conversation on the surface level. Making sure they are using a lot of leading questions in order to find out what you are willing to talk about and expose. Remember the goal for these guys are a good time, namely sex. So when speaking with them you have to be very careful in your responses to their questions.

This guy may compliment you on how good you look and how banging your body is. He may say something about your smile or your lips. He will discuss a lot of superficial things. This is a sign of what type of fisherman you are dealing with. He may be less likely to highlight how smart and kind you are. He doesn't really care because, remember he is in it just for the fun.

One thing about these type of fishermen is if the fish aren't biting or you are not buying into their charm they will move on to another location. Because they are fishing for fun they want bites really quickly. They don't have the patience of the fisherman who's fishing for food or for sport. This is also another way to detect what type of fisherman you are dealing with.

With lack of patience and little effort these fishermen usually attract women who are "starving" for attention or having the need to be desirable. If you become blinded by all the compliments and attention you will definitely become a catch for the guy who is fishing for fun.

To keep from being caught by this guy it's good to ask a lot of questions, ones that make him think. Don't allow the conversation to turn sexual. Keep the conversation on topic when he tries to change it. Don't be mesmerized by compliments. Thank him and keep talking; this type of dialogue should turn the guy who's fishing for fun away.

The next guy is the guy who's fishing for sport. This type of fisherman has a lot of patience. He has done this many times before. The guy who fishes for sports understands the need for patience the proper bait and technique. Usually this guy goes for the trophy fish. The woman, who's well dressed, has the good job, her own house, good credit, great conversation, nice car and seems beautiful.

See, for the guy who is fishing for sport, he goes for the big fish like the marlin. Marlin fishing is considered to be the pinnacle in offshore sport fishing. Most marlin fishing is done out in the deep water like the Pacific or the Atlantic ocean. A marlin fisher goes for the one's that the guys who fish for fun never will. See the sports fisherman wants to catch the fish and take it home as a trophy. This guy isn't going to just throw you back; he plans on keeping you around for a while. The sports fisherman is not afraid to spend money. It cost money to fish for sport. That's how he's able to catch trophy fish because he can throw money around to make sure he's successful. He understands the more money he spends the better he is positioned to catch the best fish. Don't be tricked because this may seem like a good thing.

How do you know if you are being pursued by a guy who's fishing for sport? This can be kind of tricky because like I said earlier this guy plans on keeping you around for a while. Guys who fish for sport usually spend a lot of time on a boat somewhere. They are always looking for the thrill of the next big catch. One way to determine if this guy is going to be committed to you or not is if you start to demand more of his time is spent with you. But, he would rather be on a boat or at a club. Chances are he is not ready to settle down and you are just a trophy for him. He likes the idea of you being on his arms at times of his convenience. He is not interested in making you a priority. He will probably just give you money and say go shopping or something and he will see you tonight. If you ever start talking about marriage or any real commitment and love he will say things like "You know I love you." "Look at all the things I do for you." He may ask "Why should we change our situation by getting married?" He says it's working for you and him, but it's really benefitting him only.

See this type of fisherman is always about the next catch. So he's always looking for something he considers bigger and better. When he feels he's found it, he will drop you like the bait in the water that he used to catch you! To avoid being caught by this type of guy let him know up front that quality time is a big priority for you, and that you just don't want money or gifts, but rather his attention. You should stick to that position; let him know that marriage to the right man is one of your goals. Usually when you start talking like this the guy who is fishing for sport will move on to the next adventure.

The final fisherman is the one who fishes for food. This guy fishes with the intent of taking you home because he understands the importance of a woman in his life. He is the guy who is not going to starve himself with lack of commitment and one night stands. He plays for keeps even though like the other two fishermen, he still has his preferences, but he is more concerned about the benefits and strength that he gains by having the right woman in his life. He wants to be able to feed off the wisdom that the right woman has and the nurturing ability that she possess. There is also the fulfillment of love making that comes from the intimacy of a loving and committed relationship. This type of fisherman doesn't fish with phony bait but he uses real bait because he feels that honesty in the beginning will save him a lot of problems in the end.

He brings honesty because he expects honesty. Usually this guy has been fishing for a while, since he fishes for food he understands the importance of providing for his family. It may even be the case that he was once the guy who fished for fun or fished for sport. Over the course of time he has learned to be patient, not pushy, forceful or demanding. He has learned over time how to catch the right fish because he understands what women really need. Not to say he is perfect because no one is, but he has the tenacity and he is open to change.

You will know this guy when you meet him because his life will just about be an open book. This is the guy I believe most women are expecting when they are little girls dreaming about being married one day. The good news is this man still exist ladies! He is looking for a woman like you to help him become everything he needs to become.

CHAPTER 2
SIGHTS SET

Men are hunters. Because of this, once a man has you in his sights he studies you for a while. He is looking at the way you are dressed, the type of friends you have and how you interact with those friends. He is listening to the conversations you are having. These things help a guy determine how he should approach you and what category he should put you in. Most men have one of three categories. The first is the booty call, then girlfriend and finally wifey material. This is why it's very important for a woman who is waiting to meet a good guy with the hopes of being married one day, to be on her A game. If you are a woman who is desirable and attractive to most men you will have to weed through the guys who are sports fishers and fun fishers to meet the guy who is fishing for food.

Women, you have the ability to ward off the wrong guy and have the category he puts you in change by your conversation and actions. Conversation is very important during the first meeting. You have to be very careful not to give the impression that you are easy or maybe it's just gonna take a little time before he gets you into bed. Remember the wrong guy's goal is sex. First off be sure not to give too much information about yourself up front. Sometimes the type and amount of information you give can help the wrong guy determine what type of bait he needs to use. Let's break down the three categories that most men place women in and the certain characteristics of each type.

The first category is the booty call; usually men place women in this category who are provocatively dressed. That's kind of obvious for this particular category, but there are times when women are well dressed and well-maintained or quiet even though they have a strong inner desire for sex. In a case like this the guy usually approaches the woman and begins to ask surface questions like how are you? What's your name or where you are from? After a little laughter and more conversation the guy will begin to ask questions that will determine what type of men she likes and what her previous relationships were like. These questions if answered the wrong way help the guy move in for more sexual questions. Then he may ask questions like how long has it been since she has been with a man? At this point the guy has already determined that this female is easy and is open for just about anything.

In these questions it's obvious the guy really doesn't care about how smart you are or if you would be a good mother to your kids one day. These questions will help you understand what this guy is after. The problem is most women just allow this type of conversation to continue either out of ignorance or by choice and then wonder why weeks later the guy is barely calling or wanting to hang out after you both had sex.

The next category is the girlfriend category. After the man has approached you and the conversation has begun he seems very nice, polite and caring. That's because he is planning on hanging out with you for a while. His plan is to take you out to dinner or maybe even to church but his goal may still be the same. The sexual encounters may go on for a while and may even turn into a long term relationship. However, at some point the excitement of having a new person around and good sex partner has to turn into the possibility of commitment, namely marriage.

At this time the guy is probably comfortable with what you guys have and the conversation of marriage will turn him off. This is why statistics tell us that courtship which is a very antiquated word today is better to enter into than dating when you are a person who is seeking commitment and marriage. We will talk more about courting and dating in a later chapter.

The next category is wifey material. Women who fall into this category with a man are women that have non-negotiables and stick to their guns. This is the woman who will not allow a man to draw her into any conversation she feels is inappropriate. She exhibits no signs of bending her own rules. These are the type of women that turn the wrong man off and turn the right man on. Women who are seeking committed relationships that can lead to marriage must have non-negotiables. Non-negotiables is a term that businesses use that mean the terms and conditions of a contract are not open for change or negotiation. The company will not budge when it comes to these non-negotiables. Non-negotiables help keep your boundaries intact when dealing with men. One of these non-negotiables should be refusal to have sex before marriage.

Studies have proven that people who live morally clean lives before marriage are less prone to infidelity afterwards. What I find today is that most people feel that sex before marriage is one of the best ways to determine if you will be compatible with your mate. I totally disagree with this thought. I believe this position is part of the reason there are about 41 percent of marriages where one or both spouses admit to infidelity, either physical or emotional. Studies found that about 70 percent of married men admitted to cheating on their wives. And about 50 to 60 percent of women admitted to having an affair. So it is very important for women to have this non-negotiable and it should be made known to a guy early on. Once you have discussed your non-negotiables leave them there. Most men will respect the fact that you have unbreakable rules. The right guy that you desire will have his own non-negotiables as well.

What I find in some cases women start out assertive, determined to follow their goals but don't follow through with them. This may be a woman who has been single for a while and starts to think that her standards are too strict. She sees her friends in relationships and starts to get anxious. Listen ladies it is very important that you stick to your guns concerning your non-negotiables. Sometimes the guy who's fishing for fun or the guy who's fishing for sport can slip past your radar. These guys will even see your non-negotiables as a challenge to see if they can get you to break them. If you give in and allow them to get you to break one of your rules, they will continue to push the envelope to see if they can get you to break more and then lose respect for you once you do. So don't budge from your non-negotiables no matter how badly you may feel, or how hard it gets. Be steadfast and unmovable when it comes to your own rules!

CHAPTER 3
THE WOUNDED ANIMAL

Normally animals that hunt usually go after the vulnerable prey. The one that maybe wounded or alone. In this situation the hunter has the upper hand and won't have to work as hard. Women who are feeling alone or have been hurt from past relationships usually become attractive prey for the wrong guy. Ladies it's important that even if you have been hurt, abandoned or feeling confused that you don't expose these wounds publicly. Keep them private at least at first, and try and seek the help you need. This will keep you from becoming trapped by the wrong guy. Now don't get me wrong - there are a lot of good guys who you can share your wounds with who won't take advantage of the situation. This could be a great guy for you, but before you try and move into anything with him be sure you are totally healed. You don't want to be the woman who hurt a great guy because your wounds were still open.

No woman or man is ready for any relationship until they are a whole and healed person. If you are not healed that puts the other person in a position to try to make you happy and whole. It's never the job of the man you're in a relationship with to make you happy. You have to be happy with yourself first. If not no matter what the other person does it will never be enough. He will always need to perform to try and fill a void that was never meant to be filled from external stimuli. So it is very important that you take time to become whole and healed from any wounds. It is very difficult to give anyone anything that you don't possess. If you don't first love yourself you will never be able to love anyone or even receive love for that matter.

Normally people who are wounded operate from a place of lust and not love. There are major differences between the two. Love gives to others without some selfish motive of personal pleasure or gain. While lust on the other hand takes from others with the selfish motive, of personal pleasure or gain. Women or men who have been wounded often look for ways to deal with the pain they may be experiencing. Often times it's through sex or bounce back relationships. Which in most cases are driven by lust. It puts an unsuspecting person in a position of being hurt or wounded because they were looking for love, but you were looking for ways to deal with your pain. Wounds take time to heal. It's nothing wrong with taking the necessary time needed to recover from past hurts in order to successfully move forward into a hopefully positive and meaningful courtship. Don't rush the process, if you do you may find yourself repeating the same mistakes and opening yourself up to be wounded again! Like the popular saying that spread throughout the nation a couple of years ago, "Ain't nobody got time for that!"

Healing From Being Wounded

Healing from a relationship gone wrong can be very difficult. I've seen situations where a person has taken close to two years to heal. Everyone's healing process is different. Healing from a broken heart is not like healing from a cut. That normally takes 1-2 weeks to heal. In a relationship where a person has really invested a lot of time or have been spiritually, emotionally, and physically invested it will take more time to bounce back from than a relationship that was just casual. According to a study published in the Journal of Positive Psychology, 71% of 155 young adults took about 3 months in order to see positive aspects from their breakup. As I stated everyone's situation is different. 11 weeks may be too short or too long depending on the circumstances of the relationship. Social media also may add to the length of recovery time due to pictures of ex's being posted all over the place. Pictures of them going out and doing things seemingly having fun without you. Social media can be used as a get even tool.

As I earlier mentioned healing can be a process. But I do believe there are some things a person can do to help with healing.

1. Take your brokenness to God. God will help any wound or pain we feel to heal properly. Cast your cares on Him because He cares for you.

2. Allow yourself to hurt or feel pain. It's human nature. Don't deny what you feel and give yourself the opportunity to process.

3. Make sure you talk to people who you can have healthy dialogue with. People who really care about you. Those who won't just tell you to get even. But folks who will give you encouragement and constructive criticism.

4. Don't move into a rebound relationship. That will only make things worse. It can possibly cause more damage and prolong your healing process.

5. Focus on you not on the other individual. Take care of you. Join a gym, get your hair and nails done. Eat healthy. Get dressed and take yourself out.

These are just a few things that can help you bounce back and get healed enough to move into a productive courtship that can lead to marriage. Being totally healed and completely moved on from past hurt is paramount when considering moving forward into a new relationship.

CHAPTER 4
THE POWER STRUGGLE

Women you must understand that you hold the power. Some men are accustomed to having women give away their power so when that wrong man approaches, he's gonna come from the assumed position that he has total control of the situation. The power women that you possess is based on your attributes, your wisdom, your compassion, your conversation, your body and the simple fact that you are a woman, plus you have a vagina. Man needs woman! The wrong guy will be driven by one thing. He won't be concerned about all the benefits you bring to his life because he's sexually driven. When men cheat on their spouse it's most always for sex. Either they feel like they are not getting what they need at home, or they have self-esteem issues and cheating makes them feel good about themselves. Cheating makes them feel in their own minds like they "still got it!" Sadly though a lot of good women get caught in the crosshair of this selfish ambition. Sex is so important to the wrong man that he is willing to risk his life for it!

I did some research on a cheaters website and what I found shocked me. I found that today it seems like everybody is cheating. The most alarming thing I found is that in countries where cheating is punishable by death, men in these countries still cheat! Now that should prove to you how much power you as a woman have. I see women every day give their power over to the wrong man and the sad thing is ladies once you give men this power and control you usually never get it back. At least not in that relationship. So there becomes a power struggle. Non-negotiables that I spoke about in chapter 2 will help you keep your power. The wrong man is going to approach you from the place of supposed power. But when you don't bite the bait you confuse the guy because you didn't feed into any inappropriate conversations and you weren't extra giddy over his compliments! Now he has to regroup and be quick on his feet. He will either come up with another approach or walk away feeling defeated, but not before he probably calls you a few names. Or suggest that you think your are all that. Or he really didn't want you anyway. See ladies you have just exposed him and saved yourself a lot of heartache because you didn't allow your power to shift. You stuck to your guns!

Shift in power usually happens when a woman in a relationship loses herself. She forgets the woman she was before she met the guy she's involved with. He becomes her god and she forgets she had a life, dreams, and goals. I've seen this happen to a lot of women. She's attracted to a guy, falls head over heels in love and loses all sense of herself. Now, instead of the guy pursuing the woman, leading her in love and romance, the woman becomes the one leading and pursuing. The woman has given away her power. Her confidence is gone along with her self-respect. Now she puts up with things she never would have before the power shifted. The guy now takes advantage of the situation and the woman. This is where lies and infidelity comes into the relationship from the guy but he still demands respect and commitment from the woman. Women, you must never forget who you are in a relationship and what you bring to the table. Never lose the confidence you had in yourself before you met him. Stick to your non-negotiables so you can hold onto the power you had before you two met. If not you will find yourself conforming to things you said you never would and you'll become a person you no longer recognize.

CHAPTER 5
THE AGGRESSIVE WOMAN

In today's society it's becoming normal to meet women who are pretty aggressive. Women who know what they want and aren't afraid to go after it. I don't always think this is a bad thing when you are talking about starting a business or women as heads of corporations. There is nothing wrong with women who take control of their lives and make a living and take the lead in society. I do however; think it can be a bad thing when dealing with relationships.

It's the natural order of things for men to be the aggressor. It's in our DNA to be hunters. Whenever you take away from a man the ability to be the aggressor and pursue you, you are setting yourself up for major disappointment. Especially if you are dealing with a guy who's a mama's boy who is used to having his mama do everything for him. This guy will welcome you being the aggressor because he's used to a woman leading and taking care of him; but trust me you will regret you ever met him sooner or later.

It's becoming popular today for the woman to even propose to the man. I've seen all over social media well-meaning women down on their knee asking a guy to marry them. In the background you will have her friends cheering her on, while not knowing she's making a grave mistake. I always wonder when I see images or videos where the woman is proposing, where is her father? No real man that I know of will ever allow his daughter to do such a thing. Call me old-fashioned but I believe the man should be the knight in shining armor that comes and rescues the woman and ask for her hand in marriage. Not the other way around.

I remember I was in a grocery store taking care of some business through Western Union and the lady who was waiting on me began to flirt with me. I was short fifty cents of the amount needed when she generously, so I thought, added the money. Then she smiled and said that I could take her out to lunch to repay her. I laughed it off trying not to make an uncomfortable situation more uncomfortable. I grabbed my receipt and told the lady goodbye and left the store. When I got into my car I began to think back to that exchange we had and how aggressive the lady was. What the lady didn't understand is that she sent a very bad message being so straight forward and aggressive. The guy who's a "fisher for sport" or "fisher for fun" would have taken advantage of that situation hook, line and sinker.

It's alright for a woman to be interested in a guy but she should never just throw herself at him leaving the guy without his need for a chase. The woman in the store didn't drop any subtle hints, smile or other body language she just went straight for it. If I were the "fisher for fun" that I was many years ago before marriage this would have been a dream situation. The young lady said I could take her to lunch but what the guy who's a "fisher for fun" would have heard was we can have sex. What he would have done probably was give her his number, not ask for her number simply because she put herself in a position to go after him, so he will let her. Then when she calls which she definitely would have he would have talked to her just to make her feel like he was interested in her a little. Then he would have set up a time to take her out, they would have went out laughed and then went back to his place. From that point on she has just become his booty call. If he's a "sports fisher" she would have become his regular booty call.

Ladies, this is why when dealing with men, being the aggressor or coming on too strong is not the best way. Once you have sex with the guy you have just dropped from a ten to a three or four in his book. The newness is gone and you have lost value before he even got to know you from the inside out. There's always an exception to the rule, but in most cases you drop in value to him and the chance of him ever wanting to really get to know you outside of your favorite sexual positions are very slim. Women it's very important that you approach the situation with men from the right position. Never too aggressively or give too much away too fast. When you do that you will never be taken seriously and you will deal with a lot of pain and disappointment. Ladies you are valuable and you are a treasure and asset to us men. Don't just give your treasure away. Make a guy dig and work for it. Anything that holds true value doesn't come easy and neither should you.

CHAPTER 6
MEN VS. WOMEN

No matter how much the rules for relationships change, one thing will always stay the same. Men are very visual creatures whether they are gay or straight. Women are more driven by emotional arousal and the need to feel protected and safe in the arms of a man. Studies have shown that 84 percent of women compared to 16 percent of men are more likely to purchase romance novels. For women it's more about that emotional connection whether truth or fantasy that stimulates them in any relationship.

Studies have also shown that men ages 25-34 are 37.2 percent more likely than 16 percent of women to purchase pornography. This further proves the point, that men are more visually stimulated than women.

Men can see something and began to be aroused and go after that object of their arousal until they have conquered it. It's easy for a man especially if he's driven by lust. On the other hand, in most cases, women want more of an emotional connection. Women also are drawn to men who seem to have great confidence and status. In today's society you see women try to take on the role of a man and act as if all they want is sex and that's it. For some women (very few) this may be true. But for the majority of women taking this position can prove to be very dangerous, because at some point it's almost impossible for you not to get emotionally involved. That's just how you are wired. However, men can play this game and never emotionally commit because they are stimulated and wired differently.

I've heard stories of women that have tried threesome's with the man they were "dating" to prove that they loved him. In most cases these situations were brought up by the man. Women are naïve to think this situation will be harmless and that the relationship will just go back to normal after the threesome. They just opened the door for major damage to the relationship and heartbreak for themselves. Once you open the door to this in your relationship the guy even though he may say "just this one time" will never want that door closed again! Women you have to outsmart him and stick to your guns. You also have to know that you would never have to prove your love to the "right guy" in this way. Men can't just put the brakes on like you and go back to normal. After you have allowed him to fulfill a wild fantasy like this, most of the time he will want more. It will only end when you decide to end the relationship and leave hurt, damaged and confused. Women don't try to play a man's game because you will never win. Stay true to yourself and stay true to how you are wired and wait on God to send you the "right guy."

CHAPTER 7
COURTING NOT DATING

The majority of people today are more aware of what it is to "date" than to court. Normally when we think of courting we think of something old fashioned that our grandparents use to do. However, courtship is actually becoming more popular today than in recent years. It's not only popular among Christians but, non-Christians as well. Many people are starting to embrace the idea that courtship is a better arrangement than dating when you are a person looking for a committed relationship that will eventually lead to marriage. Before we continue any further let's look more closely at these two terms and their definitions.

First, dating is the act of spending time with another person for fun, sex or a casual relationship.

Next, courtship is the act or art of seeking the love of someone with the intent to marry and spend the rest of your life with. It's the wooing of one person by another. Now I understand that in today's society marriage is becoming less popular and more couples are deciding to cohabitate rather than to commit to marriage altogether. It is said that one in five adults 25 years and older or about forty two million Americans have never been married. That number is up from a 1960 consensus that recorded one in ten adults have never been married. That was nine percent of all adults. However, I have discovered that marriage seems to have many benefits.

It is said that married men and women tend to be better off financially and that married people live longer, more secured and healthier lives.

Dating according to the definition that was given seems to have no real pointed goal. I remember before I was married to my now wife of fourteen years. I dated a lot of women, ironically none of those women that I dated ended up becoming my wife.

The woman that I decided to marry was the woman I courted, not dated. So both of the terms hit home with me. I've been involved in both courting and dating. I must admit I was dating for fun and sex. It wasn't until I got serious about my life and future that I decided to no longer have sex before marriage and really spent quality time building a friendship and getting to know the woman that I was truly serious about.

It is said that the divorce rate is higher among people who cohabitate or were promiscuous before marriage than of those who abstain from these types of activities. I think that one of the beautiful things about courtship and the success that it brings to a long lasting relationship is that sex in not involved. If both individuals can control themselves in the beginning I think it helps birth the strength needed to say no to sexual advances that may come from outsiders who are open to cheating with you or your spouse during your marriage.

It's not to say that the marriage will never have

problems, but courtship can help build a sturdier foundation. This foundation will help the couple remain steadfast when the storms of life come. I know there are a lot of people who are not really familiar with courtship so I want to spend some time on how to successfully court.

How to successfully Court

Courtship should only be entered into when the goal of both individuals is marriage. In courting the power is given back to the woman and puts the man in the position of having to work and win the woman. You ladies become his prize and if you really mean as much to him as he says you do he will do everything and just about anything to win you. The man is put back in the position of leader. Now I do understand that every woman is not impressed with the man's role as a leader. A lot of women today would feel just fine taking on equal responsibility and there's nothing wrong with that. It will however suit you and especially the man better that even if he isn't in control or leading to at least let him think he is especially if he's making a strong effort. As I stated earlier men normally lead in the courtship. It's the guy's role to ask the woman of his interest into the courtship and win her. Courtship is about getting to know each other's families, friends, religion, background and interest etc. Things that really matter when the goal is marriage.

When courting usually dates are more group date type of activities. Being in groups help you to avoid excessive touching and kissing that may lead to sex. In courting relationships it's good to have other friends, couples and possibly a pastor that can hold you accountable. Courting allows you a lot of time for conversation about the future and kids or career. Getting to know the person you are courting is vital. If at any point during the courtship either of you start to realize that marriage isn't the best option for you and that you should just remain friends that's okay. Just decide to end the courtship and remain cordial toward one another. The beauty of courting is it allows you to find out sooner rather than later if the person is really the one for you. In cases like these it's easier for a couple to make this type of decision and go separate ways because there was no sex involved and the emotional struggle to part ways is not a major issue like it would be in a dating relationship.

It's important when courting for the couple to decide together what will be the limits of physical intimacy. Make sure what you decide you stick to. Decide together how you will kiss and embrace. Some may decide that there will be no kissing at all. It's really up to the couple but remember the goal is to save yourself for marriage. Too much physical contact can make it tough to abstain until the wedding day. So know each other's limitations. Remember that courtship is about romance. So keep the romance alive and healthy, do all you can for one another to show your love. Then allow this romance to follow you into your marriage.

The wooing phase of courtship helps eliminate selfishness in the relationship. How you may ask? Well let's take a look at the term "wooing" and what it really means. To woo is to seek affection or love of someone in particular the opposite sex. It also means to solicit favor or approval. When the man begins to woo you he is actually putting his best foot forward and pulling out all the stops so he can win your favor or approval. He might do things like make dinner reservations, open doors, pull out chairs, etc. All this is done not from a place of insincerity but from a place of sincerity and authenticity. It's not done for sex but to prove to you that you are the woman he desires and wants to spend his life with. To me courtship is a no brainier. This wooing should continue throughout the courtship and even after he asks for your hand in marriage, which brings me to my last point.

Some courtships may be lengthy and some may be short. The most important thing is committing to remaining pure. This should help make for a strong and very successful courting relationship.

CHAPTER 8
THE LONG WAY TO A DESIGNED DESTINATION

What I find today is that everyone wants to be on the fast track. Hardly anyone wants delayed gratification. Just about everything in our society speaks instantaneous victories. But, truth be told anything that's precious and priceless usually has a major investment attached to it. In this case it's patience. A lot of relationships today are built with the materials of impatience and lack of process. Most people never court and take the time necessary to know an individual. Honestly, it can take almost a lifetime before you really know someone. But the way the divorce rate is today and the way people are able to hide behind false images. Wouldn't you want them to process correctly before entering into something as serious as marriage, which is a covenant union?

A covenant is an agreement. It also means a lifelong commitment between two parties. The greatest covenant of all is that between God and man. The next is that of a husband and his wife which incidentally speaks of the covenant of Christ and His bride, the church. We take more time researching investments and a new car we want to purchase than researching the person we want to spend our lives with. One thing I've found out about God is that in order to get His best you have to do things His way. His way is not always the quickest way but it's the most successful, empowering and equipping way to get you to your destination. He knows what's best for us. God never places more emphasis on the destination because He is concerned about the process. He knows that all the training and readiness that you endure on the journey is far more important. When God brought the children of Israel out of Egypt there was a faster way to the promise land of Canaan. However, the quicker way was through the land of the Philistines but, He knew the people weren't ready for war so He took them through the longer route to prove them and get them ready for the battles they would have to fight once they got to the place of promise. (Exodus 13:17 KJV)

See not only are you going to have to fight in your singleness, feelings of loneliness, fornication, doubt, jealousy, etc. You are also going to have to fight once you get to your destination (marriage) in order for it to be successful and be all God has ordained it to be. So take your time and be patient. Learn all you have to learn on your way. Learn to fight and be victorious and learn to trust God. You will need all that training once you arrive at your place of promise. Trust me God's got you, His word says "For I know the thoughts that I think toward you, saith the Lord, thoughts of peace and not of evil, to give you an expected end. (Jeremiah 29:11 KJV) He has not forgotten about you. Wait on Him to send the right man.

CHAPTER 9
REAL MEN

I didn't want to end this book without spending some time talking about a real man. I spent a lot of time helping you to detect the wrong man it would be amiss of me if I didn't spend at least a chapter helping you to detect the characteristics of the right one. We no longer live in a Cosby Show or Leave it to Beaver society! Today single parent homes are a new norm. It is said that of all the single parent families in the U.S., single moms make up the majority. This is not just the norm for the poor and minorities, but many others are falling into the single mom household category due to more babies being born out of wedlock. So this means you have more and more young men of all races and ethnicities growing up in households without the example of a real man present. So today real men might be a little harder to come by than decades earlier but, there are still a lot of real men out there waiting to meet the right woman. Because I've been blessed to transition from the "fisher for sport" and "fisher for fun guy" for the last fifteen or so years I've been surrounded by and mentored by so many real men. As a result of this encounter with real men I believe I am qualified at this point to list some characteristics of what I think a real man is and what he does.

First off I believe a real man loves Jesus. Any man who's able to submit his life to the authority of the Lord is a man who will be able to carry the weight and responsibility of leading a family. A real man will always take care of and provide for that which has been committed to his care. Be it his kids, wife, house, car, extended family and friends. He will also be a man who will defend and protect his family at all cost. He will be a man who respects himself and women and he will never ask you to do anything that will make you uncomfortable or force you out of character. A real man is never violent toward the people he loves; especially his wife and children. He will always provide for his children no matter if they are present with him or if he has joint custody with an ex.

A real man will never lead with an iron fist or force his will onto others. He will be gentle and loving but firm when he needs to be. His main concern will be his family above all else and he will be diligent about leaving a legacy and inheritance for the next generation. These are just a few characteristics of a real man. There are many more. It may seem like this list is unreal or unattainable but this type of man does exist. He may not have all of these areas mastered when you first meet him, but he will be striving toward mastery. That's the mindset of a real man; he wants to be the best he can be.

If you meet a guy and he's not at least secure in himself and a whole person you might want to wait until he develops the ability to know who he is. I really believe that any man who has not lived on his own for at least two years shouldn't be looking at moving into a serious courtship. When a man has the opportunity to live on his own and take care of himself, he will be more equipped to lead a family and wife without looking to the woman to be his supporter. Women, if you meet this type of guy don't rush things because of the butterflies you feel in your stomach when you are around him just give him time to develop more but, in the meantime continue to work on you. The real man you desire is available, he might not be as tall or handsome as you visualize, but don't close the door on a guy who could possibly be your soul mate waiting on someone from your fantasy who may not really exist.

QUICK TIPS

Here I want to list 7 quick tips that you can reference as needed.

1. Don't take a guy's number up front give him yours. Even If you are not interested in him. Don't just take his number with no intention of calling. Just let him know up front in a polite way that you are not interested. The man should pursue the woman not the other way around. Don't ever store his number in your phone for the first month. Wait and see where things are going first so if he decides to stop pursuing you and you are emotionally connected you won't be tempted to start pursuing him.

2. No sex before marriage- If you do have sex in most cases it will cause you to lose value to the man. It's like driving a car off the lot, as soon as you leave the showroom floor the value goes down. Once you allow a guy to drive you off the lot you will lose some of yourself. In most cases after sex that will become a guy's main motivation.

3. Make sure you are healthy- before you court. Healthy in your spirit, soul and as much as possible your body. A guy, especially the wrong guy can spot an emotionally unhealthy woman a mile away. It will cause you to be more vulnerable.

4. Don't be too aggressive- a guy will let you know how he feels. If he doesn't then he's not that interested. If you continue to be aggressive you will look desperate and the wrong guy will take it as you

want sex. Then he will begin to pursue you for sex alone and not a relationship.

5. Have non-negotiables- and don't break them. A guy will respect a woman with non-negotiables that she sticks to. Even if he leaves you alone because you won't break them his walking away is a sign that he doesn't like them but he respects you.

6. Dress for who you want- how you dress is what you get. You don't have to dress like a nun, but you don't have to dress too revealing either. If your outfit is too revealing it may attract the wrong guy. Dressing a certain way may cause the wrong guy to assume you are easy.

7. Stay open- the guy you envisioned may come in a different height, color or build. Don't get so locked into a mental image that you miss the guy that's really for you. Be open to try new things.

ABOUT THE AUTHOR

Paul Bryant is a husband, father, author and a man who loves God. His desire is for all people to live healthy and successful lives now! No matter if he's writing about relationships or evangelism, Paul's goal is to educate and equip readers with the tools necessary to be winners in every facet of life.

Paul is available for speaking engagements, women's empowerment conferences and workshops.

Contact: leander.bryant@yahoo.com

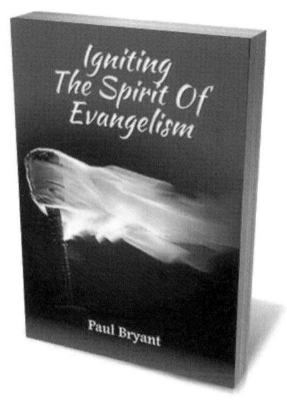

#1 on Amazon Hot New Releases
and Top 10 Amazon's Best Sellers List

Made in the USA
Lexington, KY
05 June 2017